We Can Get Along

A Child's Book of Choices

We Can Get Along

A Child's Book of Choices

By Lauren Murphy Payne, M.S.W.

Illustrations by Claudia Rohling

Free Spirit

PUBLISHING

Minneapolis, Minnesota

Printed in Singapore

Library of Congress Cataloging-in-Publication Data

Payne, Lauren Murphy, 1956–
    We can get along : a child's book of choices / by Lauren Murphy Payne ; illustrations by Claudia Rohling.
        p.   cm.
    Summary: In simple text, describes how it feels when people get along well together and when they do not, and explains that one has control over how one reacts in both kinds of situations.
    ISBN 1-57542-013-9
    1. Social interaction—Juvenile literature. 2. Interpersonal relations—Juvenile literature. 3. Choice (Psychology)—Juvenile literature. [1. Interpersonal relations.]
    I. Rohling, Claudia, 1947– ill. II. Title.
HQ784.S56P39   1997
302—dc21   96-29528
                                                                             CIP
                                                                             AC

Book design and production by MacLean & Tuminelly
Color separations, printing, and binding by Tien Wah Press, Singapore
The illustrations are done in Berol Prismacolor Markers, pen, and ink on vellum.
The type is set in ITC Berkeley Oldstyle, composed by MacLean & Tuminelly.

10 9 8 7 6 5 4 3 2 1

Free Spirit Publishing Inc.
400 First Avenue North, Suite 616
Minneapolis, Minnesota 55401
U.S.A.
(612) 338-2068
help4kids@freespirit.com

Printed in Singapore

For Aaron and Adam, my children
and Fred and Gloria, my parents.
To E.DLO.—for making me aware.

LMP

To my mother,
who told me to "climb every mountain,"
and to my dear friends
for climbing them with me. . . .
Thank you.

CR

I know lots of people
at school, in my
neighborhood, and
on the playground.
Sometimes we get along...

And sometimes we don't.

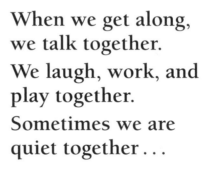

When we get along,
we talk together.
We laugh, work, and
play together.
Sometimes we are
quiet together . . .

When we get along,
I feel happy and safe.

When we don't get along,
we fight and argue.
We yell, hit, or cry.
Sometimes we say and
do mean things . . .

When we don't get along,
I feel angry and afraid.

I can remember my feelings when I am with other people.

I can remember times when I felt happy or angry, safe or afraid.

My feelings can help me . . .

To make good choices.

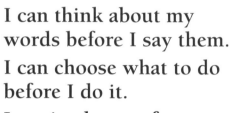

I can think about my words before I say them.

I can choose what to do before I do it.

I am in charge of my words and actions . . .

They belong to me.

I can talk and listen.
I can take turns and share.
I can help to solve problems
and work things out.
I can do my part . . .

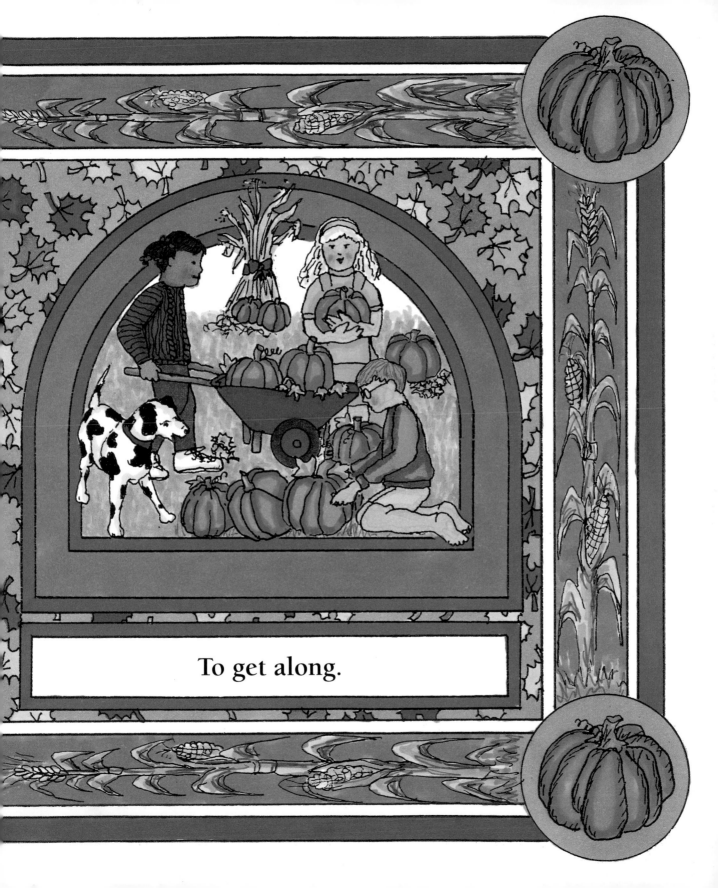

To get along.

I know how I like to be treated.

I like to be talked to and heard.

I like smiles and hugs and friendly words.

I like to be treated with kindness and respect . . .

I can choose to treat others
the way I like to be treated.

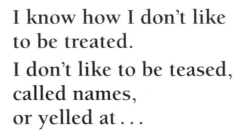

I know how I don't like
to be treated.
I don't like to be teased,
called names,
or yelled at . . .

I don't like mean words.

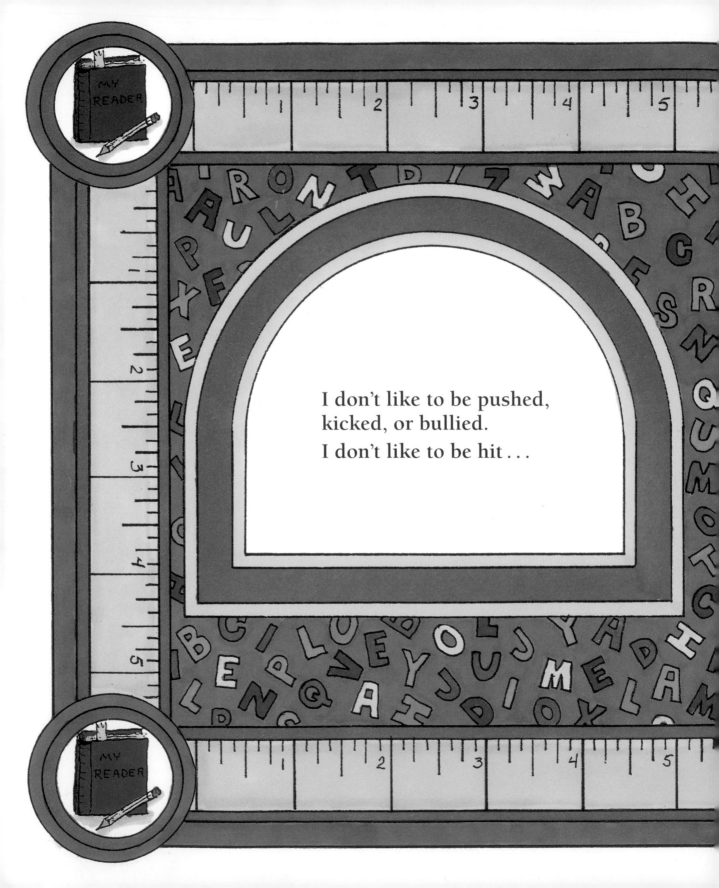

I don't like to be pushed,
kicked, or bullied.
I don't like to be hit . . .

Hitting is never okay.

These things can hurt my body and my feelings.

Sometimes I feel afraid, or I get angry.

Sometimes I want to hurt someone back . . .

CAUTION

But I can choose not to do that.

When someone hurts me, I can talk about my feelings.

I can walk away and play alone for a while.

I can ask an adult for help . . .

These are all good choices.

I can get along
with many people.

People who are like me,
and people who are not
like me.

I can learn new ideas
and try new things . . .

I can be a friend.

Friends are people
you can count on.
Friends are people
who talk to you and
listen when you talk.
Friends are fun to play with . . .

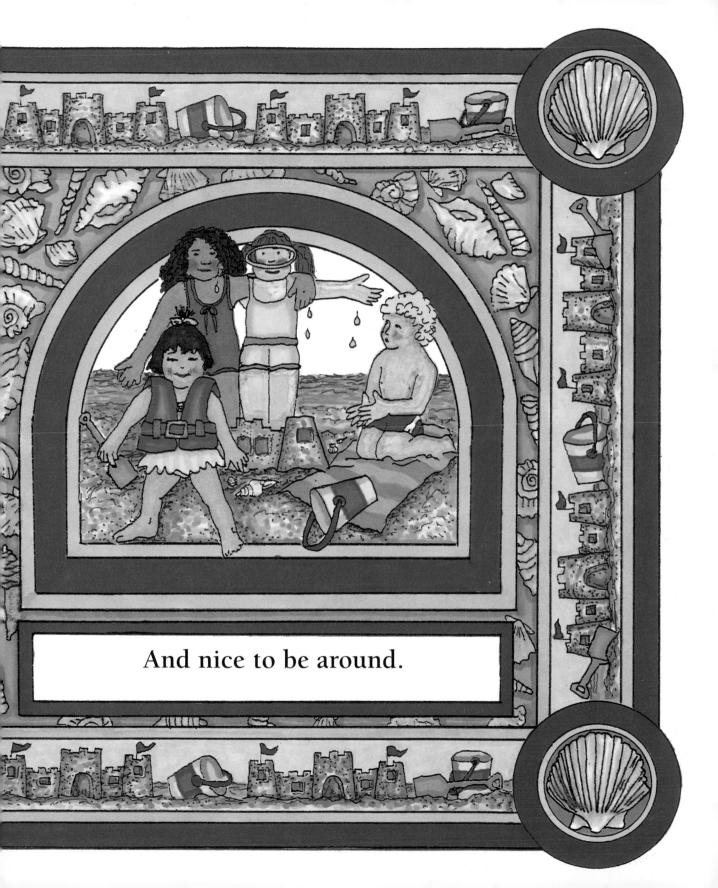

And nice to be around.

At school, in the neighborhood, and on the playground, we all have our own wants and needs.

We have our own thoughts and feelings . . .

No two people are the same.

Even though we are different, we can talk together.
We can laugh, work, and play together.
Or we can just be quiet together . . .

We can get along.

Author **Lauren Murphy Payne, M.S.W.**, is a psychotherapist in private practice. Illustrator and author **Claudia Rohling** works as an art therapist and is working on her Master's Degree. They both live in Racine, Wisconsin.

Also by the authors:
- *A Leader's Guide to We Can Get Along,* a companion to the children's book
- *Just Because I Am: A Child's Book of Affirmations*
- *A Leader's Guide to Just Because I Am*

To order or request a free catalog, please contact:

Free Spirit Publishing Inc.
400 First Avenue North, Suite 616
Minneapolis, MN 55401-1730
(800) 735-7323
(612) 338-2068
help4kids@freespirit.com